PORCUPINE PHILOSOPHY

365 Leadership Points to Ponder

PORCUPINE PHILOSOPHY

365 Leadership Points to Ponder

Steven J. Iwersen

Aurora Pointe, LLC

Published by Aurora Pointe, LLC

Porcupine Philosophy / Steven J. Iwersen. —1st ed.

ISBN 978-0-9824045-2-2

Ordering Information:

Special discounts are available on quantity purchases by corpo-
rations, associations, and others. For more information, please
contact info@steveniwersen.com or write to the "Special Sales
Department" at the address below.

Aurora Pointe, LLC
11919 Grandview St
Overland Park, KS 66213-1550

www.StevenIwersen.com

DEDICATION

To My Parents
Rev. GW and Sherry Iwersen

~

Thank you for modeling selfless leadership and giving me the gift of love, respect, and permission to explore the possibilities.

~

INTRODUCTION

LEADERS GET TO THE POINT

What do Plato, Aristotle, and a porcupine have in common?

All three will make you stop and think!

Plato is best known for his process of constant questioning and dialogue. Aristotle emphasized that happiness is a central purpose of human life. The porcupine has a few points of his own to make; but most of us would prefer to let that prickly philosopher contemplate his existence alone, somewhere in the forest.

You have probably already deduced that I am not a philosopher. I almost failed my philosophy class in college. My papers were receiving low grades - so low that I requested an appointment with the professor.

"Dr. Philo, I don't understand why I'm getting such poor scores on my papers. I am putting a great deal of effort into each one. What can I do to improve?"

He smiled and explained that, in his opinion, I was getting lost in my attempt to interpret and understand the meaning of each philosophers thesis. My papers were well-written and too serious.

Too serious?

"So, let me get this straight." I asked him, "If I don't try as hard and submit a paper that is more nonsense than logic, I'll get better grades. Is that what you're advising?"

He smiled. "Yes, that is my recommendation."

I left his office more confused than when I arrived. But, I followed his advice — turned in a paper that claimed the sky was green and the grass was pink, and I got a B+. How that paper earned a passing grade is still a mystery to me.

And yet, my professor did help me to learn a valuable lesson — that there are times in life in which we need to stop overthinking the issues and seek to simplify our understanding.

I took that philosophy and applied it to my career as a leader. The majority of my leadership roles have been in difficult circumstances in which an organization is struggling or on the verge of collapse. The external and internal conflicts have become the primary focus; and the people involved have lost sight of their strengths and opportunities. My job is to help them identify simple strategies that could help them get unstuck and back on a path of growth.

The same philosophy became a signature of my speaking style. I did not realize how influential my professor's counsel was to my development as a communicator until I started having audience members and leaders express their appreciation for how I spoke about tough topics in simple ways that were fun, memorable, and applicable.

Those types of comments are what sparked the idea of writing <u>The Porcupine Principles!</u> — a story intended to give readers a deeper understanding of leadership essentials that they can easily incorporate into their own experience and organization.

My philosophy instructor did not teach me to be glib or uncaring. He showed me that when we simplify our ideas, we can communicate with greater clarity and have a stronger likelihood of achieving better results.

The word *simplify* is defined "to make something easier to do or understand."

I believe that is the goal of effective leadership!

And to be effective in our leadership, we must have a good understanding of our principles and philosophy.

LEADERSHIP PRINCIPLES & PHILOSOPHY

Leadership principles are the paradigms that you use to guide your processes and interactions with those you lead. A *leadership philosophy* is a foundation that guides your thinking and decision-making.

One without the other makes you ineffective.

What I have witnessed first-hand is that without a strong and thoughtful leadership philosophy, leaders are easily swayed to compromise or change the principles when it serves to appease the criticism of disgruntled stakeholders.

A transformational leader relies on their leadership philosophy to keep them "level-headed" when emotions get tense, and the intentions are misunderstood. It helps them, like a compass, to stay on course in the midst of disruption and shifting objectives.

I'm frequently asked two questions:

"How do I develop a leadership philosophy?"

"What does a prickly porcupine have to do with leadership?"

Here are my answers.

You develop a leadership philosophy by taking time to think about the experiences, education, and perspectives that have shaped your convictions and values. The time you choose may be daily, weekly, or an annual weekend retreat. The point is that you intentionally evaluate *why* you lead and *how* you practice that responsibility.

The porcupine plays into this discussion because *it will make you stop and think*! It represents the complicated factors of competing goals, values, and personalities — all of which can cause us to question why we are in leadership in the first place!

Leadership can be tough. It is not easy to be in charge, especially when you have to move good people through the uncharted territory of disruption, adapt to innovations, or help them accept the reality that the mission may still be the same, but the usual methods are no longer relevant or useful. It gets even more challenging when "prickly people" in your organization keep touting that they know better.

If only you could get people to slow down long enough to think about the outstanding results that could be achieved if they would be more thoughtful of other people and considerate of their own potential. If only — you could get them to think like leaders.

Well, come to think of it - when was the last time you slowed down long enough to think about *why* and *how* you lead others? Do you have a strategic plan for developing your leadership mindset, or has your daily schedule become so crowded with expectations and interruptions that you've decided there is no time for such endeavors?

I want to encourage you to make "thoughtful leadership" a priority in your daily and weekly routine. Make it your practice to slow down, take a breath, and contemplate the subject of leadership within the context of your life and duties. It is my hope that this book will be like a porcupine on your path and make you stop and think.

~ Steven Iwersen

HOW TO USE THIS BOOK

The Porcupine Philosophy is a collection of simple thoughts, quotes, and observations about leadership gleaned from personal experience, conversations with honest-to-goodness leaders who have learned the hard way, and from some well-known leaders.

A porcupine, on average, has about 30,000 quills. Being mindful of that many points would be smart! This book does not have the same number of quotes to consider. I've decided to narrow our daily entries down to only *313 points to ponder*. The intent is to give you opportunity throughout the year to write 52 of your own reflections and thoughts.

Read the book in any way that best serves you. I'd recommend that you make it a daily habit. Read one thought and write down in the margins what comes to your mind — agreement, differing opinion, or how the idea fits in your context. Don't overthink things. Keep it simple. At the end of each week - take time to reflect on your philosophy. Write out *specific action words* of what you intend to do to strengthen your leadership influence.

Finally, don't hide away like a porcupine. Do what the great philosophers would do - engage in meaningful discussions with other leaders, so you can share your insights and learn from theirs.

PORCUPINE PHILOSOPHY

365 Leadership Points to Ponder

Steven J Iwersen

JANUARY

January 1

If you would hit the mark, you must aim a little above it: Every arrow that flies feels the attraction of earth.

Henry Wadsworth Longfellow

January 2

A unique challenge for leaders is to stay current on the issues without getting caught up in the current of the issues.

January 3

The best way to convey your viewpoint is not to tell people, but to show them.

Take them to the mountain top and let them see it for themselves.

January 4

Lead from the heart and you will win their hearts.

Lead from the head and you will lose their hearts.

January 5

Actions speak louder than words. But, be attentive to the words you speak — they become the impetus for your actions.

January 6

If you are not clear on where you are going, you will:

- stop for anything,
- detour to explore whatever looks promising,
- ask for directions from anyone who appears to know the way, but really knows nothing at all.

January 7

My Reflections and Thoughts for this Week

Actions I Will Take ~ Changes I Will Make

January 8

Try not to become a person of
success but rather a person
of value.

Albert Einstein

January 9

The words you speak today will
open or close hearts.
Be inspiring. Be careful.

Future interactions and
connections depend on how you
communicate today.

January 10

A leader becomes the point person
in a healthy organization.

They point the way and provide
clarity of direction.

The team members point to the
leader as the example.

January 11

Breakthroughs happen because of
persistence. Failures happen
because of procrastination.

January 12

There are three personal
connections that you need to
make as a leader:

Your *Head* to the Vision.
Your *Heart* to the People
Your *Hands* to the Process.

January 13

Take the lead when you see a need.

Don't wait for others to ask for
your help. Ask them to help you
create a way to meet
that need.

January 14

My Reflections and Thoughts for this Week

Actions I Will Take ~ Changes I Will Make

January 15

Anyone can steer the ship, but it takes a real leader to chart the course.

George Barna

January 16

The undoing of your leadership credibility will begin when you are unresponsive to those who attempt to communicate with you.

Being "unresponsive" is usually a sign of great illness or death.

January 17

Strong leaders do not need to do all the talking.

Your ability to *persuasively* communicate begins with your commitment to *purposefully* listen. The more you listen, the more you know what really needs to be said.

January 18

When leaders get focused on the essentials and pour themselves into the vital actions of the actual vision, momentum builds

—

excitement accelerates

—

goals are achieved.

January 19

Your integrity goes before you and
paves the way.

Deception and dishonesty lingers
like a fog after you've gone.

Live honestly and always seek
to clear the air.

January 20

Leaders who participate in the
process are more effective and
influential than those who
only direct the process.

January 21

My Reflections and Thoughts for this Week

Actions I Will Take ~ Changes I Will Make

January 22

A bad attitude is like a flat tire. You can't go anywhere till you change it.

Earl Nightingale

January 23

Lip Service at the top levels will lead to *Bad Mouthing* at the lowest levels.

Do what you say you will do.

January 24

Conflict and consideration go
hand-in-hand.

*When you face a conflict give
consideration to the issues, facts
and options.*

When you are in a conflict with a
person, giving them consideration
and seeking to understand their
perspective will help to
ease the tension.

January 25

Be confident in yourself.
Be confident in your people.
Be confident in your vision.

Confidence breeds
accomplishment!

January 26

You have no right to grumble about the conditions if you are the cause of the divisions.

January 27

I have discovered that the successes of my life depend greatly upon my commitments and the failures are directly influenced by my compromises.

January 28

My Reflections and Thoughts for this Week

Actions I Will Take ~ Changes I Will Make

January 29

Lasting leadership comes from
a personal transformation,
not a personal agenda.

Barry Banther

January 30

There are three things you should
always keep:

✓ Your word
✓ Good company
✓ A passion for learning
    new ideas.

January 31

The power of praise is the
energy of success.

Where there is no praise,
there is no passion.

FEBRUARY

February 1

Letting go of the past does not mean letting go of the vision or reason for your existence.

It means that you let go of old methods that no longer serve the purpose well.

February 2

During challenging times
people need to see that you are
willing to step ahead of them into
the prescribed strategy that is
being asked of everyone.

Leaders lead.

February 3

A reasonable transparency is
essential for establishing
a rational trust.

February 4

My Reflections and Thoughts for this Week

Actions I Will Take ~ Changes I Will Make

February 5

If your actions inspire others to dream more, learn more, do more and become more,

you are a leader.

John Quincy Adams

February 6

Your insights in the current moment help define the value of what is important.

Your foresight of what could be next is what creates the importance of what is eventually valued.

February 7

Walk in the room like you belong there. *Sit up straight* like you're been there before. *Make eye contact and smile.* Extend your hand first. When you speak, *speak up* and don't look down.

How you present yourself demonstrates to everyone else that you are truly present.

February 8

The quality of your *influence* should be evident by the way people respond when you are present in the room.

The quality of your *leadership* should be evident when you are not in the room.

February 9

Persistence aligned with
your purpose is the example
your people need to see
for them to be inspired to
reach their own potential.

February 10

My Reflections and Thoughts for this Week

Actions I Will Take ~ Changes I Will Make

February 11

Things that matter most must
never be at the mercy of things
which matter least.

Johann Wolfgang von Goethe

February 12

Circumstances (good or bad)
do not dictate nor define your
ability to lead; they are simply the
experiences that you must navigate
through as you lead the way.

February 13

Your vision is too small if the interruptions that distract you are minor and trivial.

February 14

Your reputation is measured by the quality of your relationships, not by the perception you try to convey to the world.

Your true image is reflected in your closest relationships.

February 15

"People would rather be invited
than be told.

—

It builds respect and value, and it
gives people the freedom to choose
which direction they want to go."

~ from *The Porcupine Principles!*

February 16

There will be occasions that you will choose to be silent while others ridicule you for making a decision that they know was right.

What they don't like is the inconvenience to them or the "altering" of their prestige and power.

Let the right course of action be your defense. Don't debate or defend against the foolish.

February 17

My Reflections and Thoughts for this Week

Actions I Will Take ~ Changes I Will Make

February 18

"The pessimist complains
about the wind.
The optimist expects it to change.
The leader adjusts the sails."

John C. Maxwell

February 19

Leading people through change
must be done with a sincere
appreciation for their
past experience.

Balancing a new methodology with
a respect for heritage will help
people to appreciate a new
direction.

February 20

If you must - take note of the
trivial, but don't carry it with you.

February 21

A little pain because you exercised
your skills for the purpose
of reaching a specific goal is
better than the pain that comes
when you realize you've lost
because you did nothing.

February 22

We will grow stagnant and eventually become obsolete if we are not
asking earnestly and regularly:

"How can we improve our processes, efforts, and outcomes?"

February 23

Delaying the implementation
of a plan, because of the resistance
of a few people who prefer the past,
will undermine your ability to lead
those who are looking toward
the future.

February 24

My Reflections and Thoughts for this Week

Actions I Will Take ~ Changes I Will Make

February 25

Leaders who don't listen
will eventually
be surrounded by
people who have
nothing to say.

Andy Stanley

February 26

Personal restraint practiced during
times of difficulty, misunderstand-
ing, or even attack, is the evidence
of your character and emotional
fortitude.

Reactions feed reactions.
Reasoning gives you the advantage
over the unreasonable.

February 27

Stay clear of arguments over semantics and squabbles over words. Listen carefully to the intent and it will help you understand the content.

February 28

Courage is not an option for a leader, it is an obligation.

MARCH

March 1

Dripping water is capable of
shaping a rock.

Circumstances can shape you as
well, if you choose to stay
under them.

You have a choice.
The rock does not.

March 2

Guard your life with points of
accountability and behaviors that
strengthen your values.

One compromise will lead to an
avalanche of disappointment.

March 3

My Reflections and Thoughts for this Week

Actions I Will Take ~ Changes I Will Make

March 4

Treat people as if they were what they ought to be, and you may help them to become what they are capable of being.

Johann Wolfgang von Goethe

March 5

You don't lead change.
Change happens.

You lead people in recognizing the needs and process of the change. The better people comprehend the process taking place, the more likely they will be mindful of the outcomes.

March 6

Making a decision that goes against
your desires will not be easy,
especially when it comes to the
point of seeing it through.

But a wise decision based on facts,
good counsel, and common sense is
always better than a decision based
on preferences and feelings.

March 7

Growth is not solely the result of an
inspiring dream, it comes as a result
of empowering your team.

March 8

Does your vision include opportunity for others to be involved?
If not, you are not leading.

Does your dream inspire others to
make a commitment?
If not, you are not leading.

Does your vision invite and involve
the ideas and skills of others?
*Now you're leading with
influence!*

March 9

A leader who thinks their idea
stands alone and never consults
with others for collaborative
perspective eventually becomes a
leader who is standing alone.

March 10

My Reflections and Thoughts for this Week

Actions I Will Take ~ Changes I Will Make

March 11

You are not here merely to make a living. You are here in order to enable the world to live more amply, with greater vision, with a finer spirit of hope and achievement. You are here to enrich the world, and you impoverish yourself if you forget the errand.

Woodrow Wilson

March 12

When the heart is in the right place, the head can make better decisions.

March 13

"Proactive communication and preparation helps everyone to be more successful in the beginning and prevents misdirection."

~ from *The Porcupine Principles!*

March 14

Does your vision stir your heart, wake you in the morning, and lift your spirit to face even the toughest battles *(real or imagined)* along the way?

If it does not move you, it will not move your people.

March 15

You ability to look for the good in
ideas, situations, and in people, is
your competitive advantage.

While other leaders may be
criticizing, you are creating an
environment of trust, confidence,
creativity, and courage.

March 16

Change is difficult when you're
unsure of the process.

It is close to disastrous when you
don't trust the people involved.

March 17

My Reflections and Thoughts for this Week

Actions I Will Take ~ Changes I Will Make

March 18

Example is not the main thing in
influencing others;
it is the only thing.

Albert Schweitzer

March 19

A crisis today will
appear insurmountable.

But, in the rearview mirror of
perspective it is going to be a small
thing in the past, if you step up
with integrity and take
responsibly now.

March 20

An open-minded, positive attitude lends itself to new ideas and quicker decisions.

A critical, analytical attitude leans more to tested ideas and slows down the decision process.

Finding the balance between the two is what helps a leader to make better decisions.

March 21

Trust is created with three essential ingredients:

truth, talent, and time.

March 22

The type of investment you make in developing and nurturing your top leaders will be reflected in the quality of leaders you have at the entry level.

March 23

The gap between knowing what is right and doing what is right is bridged by the following resources:

Purpose
A clear understanding of why.

Commitment
A clear declaration of your will.

Discipline
A deliberate act to follow a defined plan.

March 24

My Reflections and Thoughts for this Week

Actions I Will Take ~ Changes I Will Make

March 25

People are always blaming their circumstances for where they are. I don't believe in circumstances. The people who get on in this world are the people who get up and look for the circumstances they want, and if they can't find them, make them.

George Bernard Shaw

March 26

How do you lead
people who are in the margins?

Give them a reason to move in closer, a cause dear to them, or a reward they desire. But, the greatest reason will be a relationship that matters.

March 27

The size of your efforts will reveal the size of your dreams and goals.

March 28

Leaders are thoughtful and intentional creators of ideas.

You are either a thought-repeater or a thought-leader.

March 29

Now!

Not later.

How?

*Simply and
systematically.*

Leaders don't wait;
they create!

March 30

For clarity of mind,
write your goal
in a single line!

March 31

My Reflections and Thoughts for this Week

Actions I Will Take ~ Changes I Will Make

APRIL

April 1

You must get good at one of two things: planting in the spring or begging in the fall.

Jim Rohn

April 2

It is better to be intentional, than impulsive.

Chasing trends slows or prevents you from reaching your desired goals. It also frustrates those who follow your lead. Impulsively jumping from one idea or trick to another means that you're making it too difficult for people to finish what they've started. People have an equal need for a sense of accomplishment as they do the thrill of the chase.

April 3

Leaders who have tremendous, positive influence have well-worn shoes.

April 4

Hang time.

Professional football kickers strive to kick the ball in such a way that it "hangs" in the air for a couple of extra seconds. This gives the team an advantage to get into a better position to defend.

Hang time in business is that extra little time you give your attention to others — time to connect, honor, and appreciate them.

April 5

It is hard to be a leader if you
don't take the lead early.

Otherwise, you spend much of your
time trying to catch up.

April 6

The right actions will help you
overcome the wrong distractions!

When things change
be more proactive
and less protective!

April 7

My Reflections and Thoughts for this Week

Actions I Will Take ~ Changes I Will Make

April 8

The price of discipline is always
less than the pain of regret.

Nido Qubein

April 9

Leaders step up.
Spectators step aside.
The fearful step back.

April 10

Transparency has its risks;
but it also has tremendous
potential to open doors of
opportunity yet unrealized.

April 11

Complicated systems
will undermine confidence.

The progress you seek will only be
as strong as the process you keep.

April 12

You will not achieve what
you do not lead.

*If you desire to reach a
personal goal, you must lead yourself.*

*If you desire to persuade, you must
lead the conversation.*

Those who take the initiative and
lead will be the ones who find
the way.

April 13

If you imagine that you have succeeded all on your own, you will probably end up with only imaginary friends.

April 14

My Reflections and Thoughts for this Week

Actions I Will Take ~ Changes I Will Make

April 15

Failure is the path of
least persistence.

Unknown

April 16

It is more challenging to lead
during times of well-being and
prosperity, then it is to lead
during times of challenge.

The former risks complacency;
while the latter quickly
determines who is with you
and who is not.

April 17

You will always be empty-handed if you never ask for what you need or express your expectations.

April 18

Leaders encourage positive change.

They do not settle for protecting complacency.

April 19

"I have to be able to discern which boundaries need to be protected and never compromised, while at the same time be able to anticipate and adjust to the nuances of things not in my control."

~ from *The Porcupine Principles!*

April 20

A positive mindset must be matched with positive motion.

Otherwise, we are nothing more than wishful thinkers.

Act today!

April 21

My Reflections and Thoughts for this Week

Actions I Will Take ~ Changes I Will Make

April 22

Confidence withers
under fault finding.

John C. Maxwell

April 23

Leadership is a people-centric
endeavor. It is not a process or
project-centric objective.

You lead people first.
Nurture, resource and develop their
skills to become the leaders of the
processes and projects.

April 24

Every moment, every connection,
every conversation has a purpose.

April 25

Harping on what you don't like
will attract a choir of complainers.

Talking about your hopes and
dreams will attract an army of
the committed!

April 26

If you don't encourage a little
disruption to your way of doing
things, your way of doing things
will become obsolete.

April 27

Admitting you are wrong is like lifting the sails for fresh winds of new opportunity.

Not admitting your mistakes is like dropping anchor.

April 28

My Reflections and Thoughts for this Week

Actions I Will Take ~ Changes I Will Make

April 29

Be careful the environment you
choose, for it will shape you;
be careful the friends you choose,
for you will be like them.

W. Clement Stone

April 30

Forward progress toward a goal
depends on which pedal you
are using ... the
brake or the accelerator.

MAY

May 1

Who you choose to have as advisors in your life can make or break your influence.

Be careful. No one advisor should have such influence over you that every decision you make is really their decision and not your own.

May 2

Being *personable* will win friends
and admirers.
Being *purposeful* will win favor
and achievements.

Being both personable and purposeful
will make you a leader that has
true influence.

May 3

The goal of leadership is to
reproduce the vision,
the devotion to excellence,
and the mindset of a leader in
those who will lead the
next generation.

You are not trying to reproduce
yourself. Your obligation is to
nurture and develop the
abilities that each new leader
brings to the experience.

Leadership is the art of helping
others chart and navigate their way
to a meaningful,
reproducible leadership
experience of their own.

May 4

The people who are given access to your "inner office" (*heart and mind)* must be ones who can be trusted to:

- Respect you and each other
- Honor your values
- Tell you what you don't want to hear
- Bring meaningful information and ideas
- Be congruent in their life (in and out of the office)
- Support you publicly, challenge you privately
- Stretch you intellectually

May 5

My Reflections and Thoughts for this Week

Actions I Will Take ~ Changes I Will Make

May 6

The secret to making dreams come true?

Curiosity, confidence,
courage, and constancy.

Walt Disney

May 7

When we view respect as a
two-way street we're still going
in opposite directions.

What could be accomplished if we
chose to travel side-by-side?

May 8

Tenacity in the tedious will open doors to the tremendous!

May 9

A *dream* is not enough to
create forward progress.
A *plan* is not enough to
generate results.
To say *"I will"* won't make
it happen.

You have to do everyday what
needs to be done!
*Then the dream, the plan, and your
will can be realized.*

May 10

Children learn because they are
willing to take the risk;
while most adults won't take
the risk to learn.

May 11

Dissatisfaction is only an inch
short of expectations.

Exceeding expectations is simply
doing a good thing that someone
did not expect.

May 12

My Reflections and Thoughts for this Week

Actions I Will Take ~ Changes I Will Make

May 13

Train people well enough that they can leave. Treat them well enough that they don't want to leave.

Richard Branson

May 14

Does your dream
require a team?

If not, dream bigger!

May 15

Your greatest loss will not be in
failing to convince people to do it
your way, but discovering too late
that your best leaders went
unnoticed because you were
too busy focusing on your plan
and not being open to your people.

May 16

The way you make people feel is
the way they will feel about you.

May 17

Thoughtful leaders understand the
significance of making decisions in
the context of personal impact to
those they lead — as well as the
economic and professional
impact to the organization.

May 18

Sometimes the wisest decision
you can make is to not dabble in
work that others are better
equipped and qualified to do.

May 19

My Reflections and Thoughts for this Week

Actions I Will Take ~ Changes I Will Make

May 20

Like the captain of a ship, you should always consult with your officers before making a decision, taking their viewpoints into account. But the decisions are ultimately yours, and you must make them. If you don't, circumstances will make your decisions for you.

Laura Stack

May 21

A destination without deliberate, determined steps is nothing more than a dream.

A goal without the grind is nothing more than a wish.

May 22

It might be easy to lead passive, compliant people.

The true test of your leadership abilities will take place when you are matched with similar or stronger personalities that are more independent.

May 23

A fleeting thought
is an idea
not
acted upon.

May 24

A cherry on top of the whipped cream doesn't change the fact that a mud pie is still a mud pie.

The wrong vision and method, regardless of your confident and passionate presentation, is still wrong if the implementation disrespects the relationships and does not produce the right results.

May 25

Your history is history,
Your future is yet to be,
So make today all it is meant to be!

May 26

My Reflections and Thoughts for this Week

Actions I Will Take ~ Changes I Will Make

May 27

You can't depend on your eyes
when your imagination is
out of focus.

Mark Twain

May 28

Self-confidence works almost the
same as a thermostat in the
organization — it determines the
quality of the climate.

The difficult part is keeping the
right blend of personal humility
and professional certainty.

People want a leader who is
personable and purposeful.

May 29

What compromises have crowded into your life and business?

What is diluting or cheating you and your people from the full measure of your purpose?

Leaders clean house without apology.

May 30

If you practice what you preach, make sure that what you preach is worth practicing — because what you practice is what you produce.

If you don't set the agenda for your life, someone else will.

May 31

Your choices, both personal and professional, will cause people around you to make choices in regards to their opinion of you.

Some will judge you.
Others will join you.

Make your own choice based on personal conditions, not on popular conventions.

JUNE

June 1

Be a leader who is forthright and
prepared to give an answer to
those who ask for a reason
for the direction or decision.

Leaders who leave
people in the dark
will eventually watch
their people leave.

June 2

My Reflections and Thoughts for this Week

Actions I Will Take ~ Changes I Will Make

June 3

The first responsibility of a
leader is to define reality.
The last is to say thank you.
In between, the leader is a servant.

Max DePree

June 4

The best place to observe your
leadership influence is in the future
- as a spectator.

June 5

Dream courageously!
Plan realistically!
Act immediately!

June 6

A bold, take charge attitude does not make you a leader. A humble, kind-hearted attitude does not make you a leader.

A balance between the two *will not* make you a leader. Even though it will help to make you a better leader.

What makes you a leader is the trust people place in you to help them achieve a desired result.

June 7

Plain spoken leadership is much better than politically-correct scripted statements.

However, polite self control should always guide the words spoken plainly.

June 8

Your *intention* should be the filter by which all things gain your *attention*.

June 9

My Reflections and Thoughts for this Week

Actions I Will Take ~ Changes I Will Make

June 10

In matters of style, swim with the current; in matters of principle, stand like a rock.

Thomas Jefferson

June 11

The distractions that keep us from realizing our highest potential are not usually the unwelcome ones.

They are those that we quickly entertain because of our curiosity or because they are easier than the current task at hand.

June 12

Do what matters most - first!

Or eventually, what matters most won't get done at all.

June 13

You will have to courageously challenge the norms of a culture that does not serve the well-being of everyone involved.

Don't hesitate to call for change if it can bring justice, fairness and peace as an outcome.

Steven J Iwersen

You will lose credibility if you
concern yourself too much
with not wanting to offend or
rush people.

You must balance your respect for
others with your responsibility to
get things done.

Embracing new methods
to achieve the goals
rooted in your core
values is key to
remaining relevant.

June 16

My Reflections and Thoughts for this Week

Actions I Will Take ~ Changes I Will Make

June 17

> Don't wait for the
> perfect opportunity.
> Just take an opportunity
> and make it as perfect
> as you can.
>
> Mark Sanborn

June 18

"The best decisions come from
timely, meaningful information
and clarity of direction."

~ from *The Porcupine Principles!*

June 19

There are five essential priorities for a leader to be mindful of while serving:

Your...
- Personal well-being —
  The resolve to be responsible
- Purpose —
  The reason you lead.
- People —
  The relationships
- Process —
  The routines.
- Progress —
  The rewards.

June 20

When leadership is required of you show up early, speak up early, serve early!

June 21

Your attention to the life events
of your people will demonstrate
that their personal worth is a
part of your agenda!

June 22

Don't be so consumed with the
minutia of your work that you fail
to recognize the value of talented
people around you and the great
ideas that surface in everyday
conversations.

June 23

My Reflections and Thoughts for this Week

Actions I Will Take ~ Changes I Will Make

June 24

The most difficult thing is the decision to act, the rest is merely tenacity.

Amelia Earhart

June 25

Tough circumstances call for tough decisions and firm, determined actions.

We do what is not popular for the sake of doing what is right.

June 26

The stronger your desire to
reach your destination,
the more determined you will
be to find a way.

Do not be deterred,
be DETERMINED!

June 27

Parting company with grace,
dignity, and respect will provide
the opportunity for gracious
reunions in the future.

June 28

Give your people cause to
celebrate.

Encourage their goals, growth,
and ideas.

Create an atmosphere of positive
camaraderie and the quality of
their work will improve.

June 29

Not all change is good.

But the good we do
as a result of it
can make all
the difference.

June 30

My Reflections and Thoughts for this Week

Actions I Will Take ~ Changes I Will Make

JULY

July 1

Those who try to do something
and fail are infinitely better than
those who try to do nothing and
succeed.

Martin Lloyd Jones

July 2

Two qualities are needed in the people you have on your team —

flexibly and initiative.

July 3

A *"don't rock the boat"* attitude combined with a *"maintain the status quo"* leadership style will leave you wondering how you missed the boat.

July 4

Don't let the prickly people hold you back.

Move ahead with confidence.

July 5

Your goal as a leader is to develop
the independence and self-confidence of those who follow you.

The goal is not to make them
dependent on you!

July 6

Issues that arise are not constraints,
they are conditions.

Conditions change and frequently
do, like a rain storm. It comes and
eventually moves along. There is
nothing you can do to change the
weather and it doesn't have to stop
you from living to your potential.
You adapt to the conditions and
start carrying an umbrella.

July 7

My Reflections and Thoughts for this Week

Actions I Will Take ~ Changes I Will Make

July 8

If you stop learning today,
you stop leading tomorrow.

Howard Hendricks

July 9

Leaders are not ashamed to draw
back and regroup when the timing
for an initiative is not right.

It is better to regroup and retreat
than to rush forward and get beat.

July 10

If you fail to take advantage of the
generosity and talents of your high
performers — they will leave.

If you fail to acknowledge and
compensate the effort of your high
performers — they will leave.

If you act like you value their ideas
and input, but dismiss or ignore
their concerns — they will leave.
If your best people are leaving,
you are not leading!

July 11

Inspiration often comes when we
are in isolation.
Innovation usually comes when we
are in collaboration.

July 12

"I personally believe that our responsibility as leaders is to make two essential decisions — where we are going and how we can get out of the way."

~ from *The Porcupine Principles!*

July 13

Leaders who participate in the process are more effective and influential than those who only direct the process.

July 14

My Reflections and Thoughts for this Week

Actions I Will Take ~ Changes I Will Make

July 15

The only limit to our realization of tomorrow will be our doubts of today. Let us move forward with strong and active faith.

Franklin D. Roosevelt

July 16

Strong friends and mentors will raise you up and inspire you to be better.

Weak, trivial-minded people will seek to hold you back.

July 17

Tenacity and talent are required to achieve your goals.

Talent alone will not guarantee results.

Tenacity without the talent will only make you busy.

July 18

The secret to genuine success is to resist taking the exit right before the extra mile!

July 19

The fast track to the top
is the anomaly.

It will typically take much
longer than you think to
achieve the goals.

The hard work is the same,
either way.

July 20

Make sure that when you share an
idea with someone it is intended to
help them move ahead and not just
a boast of what you've done
in the past.

July 21

My Reflections and Thoughts for this Week

Actions I Will Take ~ Changes I Will Make

July 22

Everything comes to those who
hustle while they wait.

Thomas Edison

July 23

A growth mindset must be
accompanied by growth actions
if there is to be any growth at all.

July 24

What you can imagine
and what you will realize
are brought together by
what you actualize.

July 25

The leader who lays the foundation
may not be remembered by future
generations, but the fact that
there are future generations
is the reward.

July 26

The strength of your bottom line is
directly related to the strength of
your follow through.

July 27

Consistency is the avenue
to results.

Devotion is the engine to
your desires.

Action is the vehicle that moves
you to success.

July 28

My Reflections and Thoughts for this Week

Actions I Will Take ~ Changes I Will Make

July 29

Be faithful in small things because
it is in them that your
strength lies.

Mother Teresa

July 30

A breakthrough
is a result of
your commitment
and effort to
push through!

July 31

Sustainable success comes one step at a time.

- The mile is not traveled in one giant step.
- A wide river is not crossed in one leap.
- The moon was not reached in a single day.
- A successful life comes a day at a time.

Make the most and
best of the day.

AUGUST

August 1

Lessons I learned about leadership on the playground:

1) When you take the lead you are perceived as a leader.
2) You take the lead by seeing a need, offering a solution.
3) Taking the lead is not a forceful thing, but an act of invitation — you invite others to be a part of your idea.
4) Not everyone is interested or wants to be involved. Play with those who want to play.
5) Taking the lead is how you initiate the coming together. Sharing the lead is how you stay together.
6) Playing makes the community stronger. Playing against a goal is better than competing against each other.
7) Leaders celebrate successes — the individual and group successes.

August 2

The *distractions* that keep you from your *priority actions* become the grave you dig for missed opportunities.

August 3

"When people know where they stand, they typically have more confidence and freedom to take the steps toward where they need to go. Or, in some situations, to have the wisdom to know when to step back."

~ from *The Porcupine Principles!*

August 4

My Reflections and Thoughts for this Week

Actions I Will Take ~ Changes I Will Make

August 5

The vision must be followed
by the venture.
It is not enough to stare up the
steps — we must step up the steps.

Vance Havner

August 6

Do not let your need for *Plan B* to
be activated by the result of not
giving your best effort to *Plan A*.

If you are giving more attention to
the details of your contingency
plan, you are diluting the very energy and creativity needed for the
success of your true game plan.

August 7

This is how you accomplish your
best results in less time:

Do one thing...

Do one thing with
		complete focus...

Do one thing with
		complete focus
			until finished.

August 8

The completion of your
possibilities always begins
with a commitment to
your potential.

August 9

Lean times bring about one of
two mindsets -
poverty or progressiveness.

A person who settles for a poverty
mindset resigns themselves to a life
of lacking and potential
laziness.

Those who choose a progressive
mindset rally themselves to a life of
innovation and eventual increase.

August 10

It may be necessary to change
tactics along the way, but be careful
that you don't change the mission
or you may destroy the trust
of your people.

August 11

My Reflections and Thoughts for this Week

Actions I Will Take ~ Changes I Will Make

August 12

Do nothing out of
selfish ambition or vain conceit.
Rather, in humility value others
above yourselves.

Philippians 2:3

August 13

It is possible to appear that you are
leading from a position of
collaboration and in reality be
functioning in a vacuum.
Pretending to be genuinely interested in others ideas while already
having made up your mind is not
collaboration, it is conniving.

August 14

Quality leadership is like walking a tightrope.

One foot in front of the other.

The back foot is supporting your weight. This represents the present.

The forward foot reaches out to establish a new foothold. This represents your future.

You must keep present until it is time to shift your weight to the future, at which time you become present again.

August 15

The view out of your window
is not nearly as important as
the life view that you imagine in
your heart and mind.

August 16

Organizations rise to the level of
the quality, expectations, and
example of the leader.

The organization will be mediocre
if you are controlling and focused
on the minutia. The organization
will thrive if you focus on higher
expectations and building other
leaders who can raise the quality
and experience of the team.

August 17

If you're constantly
dwelling on your past,
you will be walking
backward into the future
and will miss your very
best opportunities
because you won't
see them coming!

August 18

My Reflections and Thoughts for this Week

Actions I Will Take ~ Changes I Will Make

August 19

The leader is the one who climbs
the tallest tree, surveys the entire

situation, and yells, 'Wrong jungle!'

Stephen Covey

August 20

Don't give in to the demands of
people who won't even make
the effort to listen to your
purpose and vision.

August 21

"The best way to inspire others to improve their performance is by giving them the parameters up front and the permission to apply their potential with that context."

~ from *The Porcupine Principles!*

August 22

It does not cost
to dream.
But it will cost
to execute.

August 23

If something can be resolved
quickly, deal with it.

If it cannot be resolved quickly,
schedule it.

If it cannot be mutually resolved
at all - let it go.

August 24

Envisioning and believing in
positive results is not a luxury,
it is a necessity. It gets you moving
when you are weary. It inspires
fresh ideas when everything else is
worn and tired. Your belief in what
you do, and how it will eventually
come to be, is your fuel for each
moment and the foundation for
creating a preferred future.

August 25

My Reflections and Thoughts for this Week

Actions I Will Take ~ Changes I Will Make

August 26

Leadership consists of nothing but
taking responsibility for everything that goes wrong and giving
your subordinates credit for
everything that goes well.

Dwight D. Eisenhower

August 27

Frustration and anger is a costly
distraction to a leaders
effectiveness.

It burns up too much
intellectual and emotional focus;
robbing us of our time and abilities.

August 28

If you don't learn from your
mistakes and make the corrections
necessary for improvement,
you will not have credibility to talk
to others about their mistakes.

August 29

It is important to hear and to heed
the counsel of leaders who have
served before you.

Balancing out your decisions with a
full understanding of your past and
your potential is wise.

August 30

You either take the risk to forge
ahead into the future or you take a
seat and watch as someone else
leads the way!

August 31

What would you do differently
today if you were the CEO
of a company 20x the size of
your current organization?

Do that now!

SEPTEMBER

September 1

My Reflections and Thoughts for this Week

Actions I Will Take ~ Changes I Will Make

September 2

A person who wants to lead the
orchestra must turn their back
on the crowd.

Max Lucado

September 3

Cast a strong vision of where you
want to lead.

Communicate why you want others
to go there with you.

Call for a commitment.

Collaborate with those that
join you.

September 4

Leadership is not always
convenient. It comes with
unexpected challenges,
conflicts, and interruptions.

Your character and commitment is
strengthened when you work
through the inconvenient.

September 5

The quicker you get to the point,
the quicker your people can get
to the act of problem-solving and
hopefully the solution.

September 6

It is amazing how quickly a
group of people can generate
creative ideas when they are faced
with the urgency of a deadline
or an emergency.
Lead with a sense of urgency.

September 7

There are three indicators of a
strong, effective leader:

- Diligent effort and use of your
  talents.
- Disciplined thinking and focus.
- Devotion to a cause bigger than
  yourself.

September 8

My Reflections and Thoughts for this Week

Actions I Will Take ~ Changes I Will Make

September 9

To succeed, jump as quickly at
opportunities as you do
at conclusions.

Benjamin Franklin

September 10

Seeking advice from only those
who agree with you is not a wise
course of action.

Hearing the advice of neutral and
alternative perspectives gives you a
greater understanding of the issues.

September 11

There will times when you will be called upon to sacrifice your own comforts and preferences for the good of your team and organization.

Your commitment is measured by how much comfort you are willing to give up.

September 12

Every decision you make impacts someone you've never met and may never know.

September 13

Have you ever lost or misplaced something valuable or precious to you? A family keepsake? Your cell phone?

Do you give as much effort and attention to your work as you do trying to find something you've lost?

September 14

If you can only be kind and courteous to those you get along with or hope to do business with, then is your kindness and courtesy truly genuine?

September 15

My Reflections and Thoughts for this Week

Actions I Will Take ~ Changes I Will Make

September 16

Plant seeds of expectation in your
mind; cultivate thoughts that
anticipate achievement.
Believe in yourself as being capable
of overcoming all obstacles
and weaknesses.

Norman Vincent Peale

September 17

If you don't determine the
direction, someone else will.

If you don't take the lead — *and
actually lead* — someone
will take it from you.

September 18

Consider the attractiveness
of your vision.

If it repels strong people and at-
tracts weak, dependent people,
you don't have a vision,
you have a control issue.

September 19

How you grow depends on
what you know.

September 20

Don't force what you know
is not ready.

But, don't delay what you know
is not perfect.

September 21

If you are hoping for forward motion in your life, don't wait for the "right" emotion to make your move.

The feelings will come and go, but daily discipline is how you reach your goals.

September 22

My Reflections and Thoughts for this Week

Actions I Will Take ~ Changes I Will Make

September 23

Before you are a leader,
success is all about
growing yourself.

When you become a leader,
success is all about growing others.

Jack Welch

September 24

A leader must not be hesitant to
step up and intervene when minor
issues are unresolved.

It helps to keep a minor matter
from becoming a major concern;
and it helps to establish trust
and credibility.

September 25

A first impression is valuable.

But it is the impression people have after knowing you for many years that truly matters!

September 26

Your confidence balanced with a healthy dose of humility will draw the right people to you.

Arrogance and bravado will win you a following of self righteous, ego-driven people — all of whom will fall away the moment you stop winning.

On the other hand, a humble confident leader will find purpose-driven people standing by their side, even in moments of struggle or loss.

September 27

Influence comes before an invitation.

A person must believe in you if they are going to accept any invitation to engage, listen, or follow.

In sales, the prospect has to believe that you have something that might help them.

In management, the employee has to believe that you are competent and caring.

In leadership, the people you lead have to believe that you are trustworthy and capable.

When belief is established you can make your request.

September 28

When legacy has become more important than leadership, is the leader truly leading?

When your concern for reputation and legacy supersedes your responsibilities, you are portraying yourself as a leader of personal agenda and not a leader of people.

September 29

My Reflections and Thoughts for this Week

Actions I Will Take ~ Changes I Will Make

September 30

It is no use saying
'we are doing our best.'
You have got to
succeed in doing
what is necessary.

Winston Churchill

OCTOBER

October 1

"The most challenging discipline for us is to look at the reactions not as a problem, but as an opportunity to meet a need."

~ from *The Porcupine Principles!*

October 2

Your viewpoint and understanding of the current circumstances will not be clear if you're looking at them through *"leadership lenses"* you used ten or twenty years ago.

Things have changed. So have you.

October 3

If you are worried about the appearances of living by your convictions and doing the right thing, you will miss the opportunities to do good because you value people's opinions more than your personal values.

October 4

You have to do
what you don't like,
in order to do
what you love.

October 5

Don't rush to judgment.
Don't rush to a decision.

Determine your parameters and
expectations in advance.
Then determine if the matter at
hand fits within those standards.

This is how you become decisive
when you need to make
decisions quickly.

October 6

My Reflections and Thoughts for this Week

Actions I Will Take ~ Changes I Will Make

October 7

No man will make a great leader
who wants to do it all himself or
get all the credit for doing it.

Andrew Carnegie

October 8

You may have limited authority
in your current role, but you still
have unlimited influence on
those around you.

Be positive!

October 9

Your leadership effectiveness will
be greatly improved by your ability
to assess the need for the type of
leader your organization calls for at
any given season.

Does it need a
cheerleader,
a firefighter,
or a coach?

October 10

Your pet projects should not come
before mission-essential projects.

October 11

Your "executive presence"
is greatly enhanced
by your ability to
be present and
to execute.

October 12

You show your leadership strength
most in those moments when you
listen completely to good people on
your team and then make adjust-
ments based on their ideas and
counsel.

You show leadership stupidity
when you don't listen and force
your will, in spite of the fact that
your best people are jumping ship!

October 13

My Reflections and Thoughts for this Week

Actions I Will Take ~ Changes I Will Make

October 14

> We are what we
> repeatedly do.
> Excellence, then,
> is not an act,
> but a habit.
>
> Aristotle

October 15

Getting the right results in a timely way is your commitment.

You will have to move ahead without some people because of their delays or indecision.

October 16

We are often told to keep our eyes
on the goal. But that is not
always possible.

So, keep your heart on the goal and
your eyes on your next step.

Forward progress will bring you to
a victorious finish.

October 17

The more well read
you become,
the more well thought
you will be.

October 18

Do what you know needs to be done, no matter what.

✓ Don't feel like it.
  Do it anyway.
✓ Rushed for time.
  Do it anyway.
✓ Other things to do.
  Do it anyway.
✓ Obstacles in the way.
  Do it anyway.

When you do it anyway,
it becomes your way.

Consistency leads to
credibility.

October 19

Reaching the top of the mountain cannot be accomplished if you are trying to get there by traveling two or three different trails at the same time. You cannot physically walk on three paths simultaneously.

You must choose and commit to one path.

The same is true for reaching your goals. The most wise plan is to commit to one course of action, one path, one business model and follow through.

October 20

My Reflections and Thoughts for this Week

Actions I Will Take ~ Changes I Will Make

October 21

Great leaders are almost always
great simplifiers, who can
cut through argument,
debate and doubt to offer
a solution everybody can
understand.

Colin Powell

October 22

If your strategy is reactionary and
propping up the status quo,
you can count on your best
customers, talent, and
volunteers to go.

October 23

*A rash decision is the result
of rushed thinking.*

Gather all the information you can.
Then slow down briefly. Five min-
utes of quiet reflection could be the
buffer of protection that keeps you
from a poor choice. Allow your
conscience a little time to "speak"
to the issues.

*Information balanced with
intuition can lead to a
better direction.*

October 24

Daily actions will not make
a better future if you don't make
better your daily actions.

October 25

Habits can create a path to
greatness or can undermine and
destroy your desired outcomes.

Examine your habits and make sure
they align to your vision.

October 26

Admirable success comes as a result
of thoughtful, long-term planning
and wise short-term decisions.

October 27

My Reflections and Thoughts for this Week

Actions I Will Take ~ Changes I Will Make

October 28

Far better it is to dare mighty things, to win glorious triumphs, even though checkered by failure, than to take rank with those poor spirits who neither enjoy much nor suffer much, because they live in the gray twilight that knows neither victory nor defeat.

Theodore Roosevelt

October 29

Why we lead is significantly more important than how we lead.

How we lead quickly reveals to others why we lead.

October 30

Silence in negotiations can be a good tool for persuasion.

Silence in conflict can help defuse tension and help you hear the real needs.

Silence on communicating your vision for the company is a step toward failure.

October 31

What we call hard work is only hard in the beginning.

When we learn how to do it well and do it frequently enough to be proficient, it becomes routine and natural.

NOVEMBER

November 1

Set a goal, Schedule it!

A goal without a date is only a wish.
*You may as well throw money
in a well.*

Well... I could've.
Well... I should've.
Well... It wasn't the right time.
Well... If only.

November 2

Viability
+ Visibility
x Humility

Positive Influence

Viability = Capable of
getting things done.

Visibility = Capable of
portraying an image or
attracting attention.

Humility = Confident, not
conceited. Capable of being
comfortable with any
group of people.

November 3

My Reflections and Thoughts for this Week

Actions I Will Take ~ Changes I Will Make

November 4

A rock pile ceases to be a rock pile the moment a single man contemplates it, bearing within him the image of a cathedral.

Antoine de Saint-Exupéry

November 5

You cannot let the history of your organizational story be the script for the future.

November 6

Your motive to be a leader
should *not* be to rise to a
position of greatness.

Your motive should be to help
others rise up to their
greatest potential.

November 7

Two things need to be considered
before initiating a big change.

1) Everyone needs time to get ready
and prepared for the next steps.

2) Not everyone will stay with you
after the change, but if you lead
well they will help to make the
change happen.

November 8

The devotion and effort you give to
your work when no one is looking
will be the standard of quality
evident to all who see you
at work in public.

November 9

Double vision limits our ability to
move forward with confidence.
Competing views, opinions, or
obligations will hold you back.

Get clear on your singular vision
and direction. The moment you do,
a tremendous energy and
courageous spirit will emerge,
allowing you to move
ahead confidently.

November 10

My Reflections and Thoughts for this Week

Actions I Will Take ~ Changes I Will Make

November 11

Better to do something imperfectly
than to do nothing flawlessly.

Robert H. Schuller

November 12

Action taken early will spare
you the frustration and
disappointment of being unable
to take the preferred actions later.

November 13

There are three time frames that must be kept in mind as you lead.

- Anticipating the *future*.
- Stabilizing the *present* moment
- Respecting the *past*.

Every decision is influenced and, in turn, influences each of these "times" in an organization.

November 14

You can't change what is past, but you can pass on what you learn from the change.

November 15

A time of personal introspection will help to clarify your personal:

Expectations
What you insist upon and aspire to become.

Exceptions
What you are distracted by or willing to compromise.

November 16

What you exercise you strengthen.

- Exercise patience
- Exercise reasoning and strategic thinking
- Exercise slow to speak, slow to become angry
- Exercise love and serving
- Exercise gratitude
- Exercise working on your highest priorities first
- Exercise being attentive to others
- Exercise good judgement
- Exercise respect
- Exercise silence
- Exercise faith

The stronger your character and skills become, the greater your confidence and influence.

November 17

My Reflections and Thoughts for this Week

Actions I Will Take ~ Changes I Will Make

November 18

> Leadership is practiced not so
> much in words as in attitude
> and in actions.
>
> Harold S. Geneen

November 19

*"It is better to manage
the conversations,
not the confrontations."*

~ from *The Porcupine Principles!*

November 20

Failure is not the end of your story. It may appear to be a large public embarrassment, but that's because you're looking at it through a magnifying glass. By comparison, the rest of the world sees your failures as quite small. The people who are truly interested in your failure are looking at it through a peep hole.

It is soon disregarded for the next fascinating mistake made by someone else. The only one who is dwelling on it is you. Go ahead - examine the failure. Find what you can learn. Then put down that magnifier and focus on the opportunities you have today — opportunities to make corrections and to move on!

November 21

Executive leadership is not an invitation to be exclusive.

It is a position that requires your utmost effort to be inclusive and in touch with those who are influencing the mission at the forefront of the organization.

November 22

Your work ethic will be proven by your work habits.

Consistency contributes to congruency.

November 23

Intention determines the quality
of your attention.

The more committed you are to a
desired outcome, the more
disciplined you will be in the
behaviors necessary to accomplish
that outcome.

Your intention will inspire
innovation as you devote yourself
to achieving what others think
is impossible.

November 24

My Reflections and Thoughts for this Week

Actions I Will Take ~ Changes I Will Make

November 25

There are two levers for
moving men —
interest and fear.

Napoleon Bonaparte

November 26

The greatest testament to your
influence is that your organization
and team continues to function and
grow in your absence.

A shared vision and process that is
embraced by everyone show that
the health of the organization does
not depend upon one person
or personality.

November 27

When you are leading leaders —
don't waste time trying to cut out
a path in the wilderness for
them to follow.

Just point the way in which to go
and let them blaze their own trail.

November 28

The balance of your life is not
determined by the balance of your
bank account, but by the balance of
your priorities.

*For where your treasure is,
there your heart will be also.*

November 29

There are five types of people who are on your team:

1) People who listen and forget.
2) People who listen and remember, but never act.
3) People who listen and agree, but wait for someone else to act first.
4) People who listen, disagree, and do their own thing.
5) People who listen, understand, and do everything they can.

November 30

There will be moments that you are
providing what people have said
they exactly want, only to have the
same people put up considerable
resistance and roadblocks. Because
they eventually discover what they
thought was wanted means having
to give up comforts of what
they already have.

DECEMBER

December 1

My Reflections and Thoughts for this Week

Actions I Will Take ~ Changes I Will Make

December 2

Where there is no vision,
the people perish.

Proverbs 29:18

December 3

The size of your vision, and your
daily actions in relation to that
vision, will determine the size of
your influence.

Think small, be small.
Dream big, be big!

December 4

When you work like you own it...
you will own it!

December 5

Leaders who make decisions
quickly are demonstrating
one of two things:

Decision-making based on
knowledge and
experience

vs

Deciding based on ego
and expediency.

December 6

You may or may not want to be in charge. And yet, you'll find within yourself a stirring that pulls you toward that very thing we call leadership. It is in you — the gifting, an ability, a call. When you step up and into that ability, you'll find the strength and resources you need converging into those moments and providing what is necessary to carry out the mission.

People who appeared not to be ready to move forward will step up and offer to help. All that was needed for a group to rise to the occasion was your courage to lead. Your gift to others is the spark that lights the blaze of desire and strength to strive for a worthy goal.

December 7

Do not delay what
you can do today.

Tomorrow may not have enough
hours to accommodate
what you choose to
procrastinate!

December 8

My Reflections and Thoughts for this Week

Actions I Will Take ~ Changes I Will Make

December 9

Don't be afraid to give up the good
to go for the great.

John D. Rockefeller

December 10

A day full of activity does not
guarantee achievement of your
highest goals.

The apple at the top of the tree will
never be reached if you spend your
whole day picking only the
low hanging fruit.

December 11

There will be times that you need to take the initiative to acknowledge and accept responsibility for mistakes of the organization. This will help to reset the focus on correcting the issues and getting things done.

However, don't be quick to take responsibility for vindictive, self-serving, or distracting accusations of people who are only on a mission to drag you down.

Your people need you to show a little backbone in those times.

December 12

Leadership calls
for the strength
to say no.

December 13

It is irresponsible to make people feel shamed or disloyal if they raise questions when the organization is not growing. Their concern is not an affront to you personally. It is a desire to be part of a solution.

A leader who disguises failure in the cloak of "new methodology" is typically hiding the reality of decline and is not concerned about the growth of others, but is attempting to protect their own image.

December 14

The signature of an
excellent leader is not just the name
they write at the end of a letter — it
is the story people tell of them
when they are gone.

December 15

My Reflections and Thoughts for this Week

Actions I Will Take ~ Changes I Will Make

December 16

Do not go where the path may lead,
go instead where there is no
path and leave a trail.

Ralph Waldo Emerson

December 17

Gain information, seek ideas,
gather opinions.
But always make the effort to draw
your own conclusions and develop
your own original thoughts.

A copy cat leader is only as deep as
someone else's next big idea!

December 18

"The fastest way to get off to a good start with a person who is usually defensive or negative is to show them that you are willing to sit down and listen to them ... An expression of respect could create a willingness on their part to work with you. "

~ from *The Porcupine Principles!*

December 19

Leaders prepare not only for the immediate tasks and mission, but also for the transition. Prepare your team to receive your responsibilities when you should no longer lead.

December 20

The growth of your organization depends heavily upon the value of your vision and the effectiveness of the methods. If the cost of doing business exceeds the value of the vision - you fail.

You must keep your attention on the expense of execution, while at the same time keep watch on communicating a vision that inspires creativity and profitability.

December 21

A leader who cannot think for themselves and only regurgitates expressions drilled into them by other leaders is not leading.

They are only mimicking their mentors.

December 22

My Reflections and Thoughts for this Week

Actions I Will Take ~ Changes I Will Make

December 23

Success means doing the best we
can with what we have.

Success is the doing,
not the getting;
in the trying, not the triumph.

Success is a personal standard,
reaching for the highest that is in
us, becoming all that we can be.

Zig Ziglar

December 24

The true measure of your success
as a leader is not how many people
you can attract, but how many
people you can ask to help you in
the middle of the night.

December 25

The extent to which you *receive* is proportionate to the extent of how you *ask*.

The measurement of what you *achieve* is determined by the measurement of how you *serve*.

December 26

Your integrity causes your interactions with people to rise to a higher level.

A commitment becomes an obligation that cannot be compromised.

We need to make more commitments to ourselves.

December 27

"Persuasion can only happen when people have a clear sense of direction and the best information at any given moment."

~ from *The Porcupine Principles!*

December 28

A leaders role is to work in ways that make the conditions of a situation better. In times of disagreement, be an example of respect — guard your words, never put others down, and find a way to lift others up by seeking the best in their ideas or concerns.

December 29

The longevity of your leadership depends on the attention you give to:

- The Relationships in your life - *both personal and professional.*
- Your Health
- Intellectual pursuits, and
- Your emotional well-being.

December 30

The path ahead of you is not there
to simply view and admire;
it exists to be walked upon as you
reach for what you aspire.

December 31

My Reflections and Thoughts for this Week

Actions I Will Take ~ Changes I Will Make

About the Author

Steven Iwersen's influence as a speaker and writer in the field of leadership has been far-reaching. His ideas and approach to creating a leadership culture and navigating leadership challenges are featured in his high-energy keynotes for corporate clients, emerging companies and associations.

He is the founder and owner of Aurora Pointe, LLC, a leadership development and training company. He started the company in 2006 after having served for 25 years in leadership roles within business, associations and the ministry.

He is the author of Porcupine Philosophy: 365 Leadership Points to Ponder, The Porcupine Principles (2017), and Unplugged: Mindfulness and the Law (2016), coauthored with Joel Oster.

Steven Iwersen is a Certified Speaking Professional (CSP) and has been very involved with the National Speakers Association. He served the association in many capacities including Chairperson of the National Chapter Leadership Committee and Co-Host for "Voices of Experience" the association's audio & video magazine.

Steven is married, the father to three grown children, and is "Afi" (*Icelandic for Grandpa*) to seven wonderful grandkids. He makes his home in the Kansas City area.

Consider how Steven Iwersen can help you or your organization by having him speak at your next company meeting or conference. His creative, energetic, and highly-interactive programs can be presented as a keynote or training format.

To learn more, visit www.StevenIwersen.com You can also reach him at the below connections:

PHONE: 913-406-3824
Email: info@StevenIwersen.com
Facebook: www.facebook.com/ThePorcupineSpeaker/
LinkedIn: www.linkedin.com/in/steveniwersen/

www.ingramcontent.com/pod-product-compliance
Lightning Source LLC
Chambersburg PA
CBHW071639200326
41519CB00012BA/2351